Test your

Leadership
Skills

BRIAN O'NEILL

Series editors: GARETH LEWIS & GENE CROZIER

Hodder & Stoughton

A MEMBER OF THE HODDER HEADLINE GROUP

To the three women in my life: Alice, my mother, for her inspiration, Liz, my wife, for her example as a practising leader, and Kate, my daughter, for her helpful editing.

Orders: please contact Bookpoint Ltd, 39 Milton Park, Abingdon, Oxon OX14 4TD. Telephone: (44) 01235 400414, Fax: (44) 01235 400454. Lines are open from 9.00 – 6.00, Monday to Saturday, with a 24 hour message answering service. Email address: orders@bookpoint.co.uk

British Library Cataloguing in Publication Data
A catalogue record for this title is available from The British Library

ISBN 0 340 782080

First published 2000
Impression number   10 9 8 7 6 5 4 3 2 1
Year   2004 2003 2002 2001 2000

Typeset by Fakenham Photosetting Limited, Fakenham, Norfolk.
Printed in Great Britain for Hodder & Stoughton Education, a division of Hodder Headline Plc, 338 Euston Road, London NW1 3BH by Cox & Wyman Ltd, Reading, Berkshire.

Contents

Introduction
What's in it for you

Leadership is a fact of everyone's life. Some of us would quite like to be leaders – and most who are want to do it better. The difficulty is that 'leadership' is such a nebulous thing. We recognise it when we see it in action, but don't ask us to define what it is.

This book helps to remedy that. It provides ideas for you to purpose-build your own model of leadership. Not someone else's model, because their experience, aspirations and circumstances are not the same as yours. It has to be *your* model.

Constructing and using the model will help you to be an outstanding leader. You will be able to use it:

- to decide if being a leader is right for you and how to become one if it is
- to guide your day-to-day approach as a leader – 'how should I decide, how should I act?'
- to measure yourself and your performance – 'how am I doing?'
- to develop ideas and direction on your self-development – 'how do I want to evolve as a leader?'

The plan and building materials

So what does it take to be a truly effective leader? This is explained in the six chapters:

1. *A model of leadership.* Overview and some key concepts.
2. *The right stuff.* Have enough of the qualities that give leaders their edge.
3. *Take people with you.* Those you lead must *want* to be led – win their commitment.
4. *The right place, the right time.* Pick situations favouring your brand of leadership.
5. *Star teams.* Deliver results through serious teambuilding and teamworking.
6. *Aspirations for the future.* Looking forward, being the leader you wish to be.

In each chapter you will find questions, checklists, mini-questionnaires and other exercises. These are the tools for working the elements into a shape that suits you. And in the appendix you will find some helpful references and information sources.

To draw maximum benefit from the book:

- question what you read
- highlight the interesting bits and the bits you disagree with
- do the exercises and reflect on your answers
- make notes of key points at the end of each chapter
- discuss them with your partner or mentor.

A model of leadership

This introductory chapter focuses on:

- what leadership means; and
- where you find it.

Your ideas about leadership

? **Test Yourself**

Place a tick between each pair of beliefs to indicate how strongly you agree with one side or the other.

Beliefs about leadership

1 Leadership is inborn: you either have it or you don't. ☐ ☐ ☐ ☐ ☐ You can learn to be a leader.

2 Leaders are heroic individuals. ☐ ☐ ☐ ☐ ☐ Leaders are ordinary people.

3 Leaders are found mostly in the top echelons. ☐ ☐ ☐ ☐ ☐ Leaders are distributed throughout the organisation.

4 Leaders are charismatic. ☐ ☐ ☐ ☐ ☐ Leaders can be quite dull.

5 Tough guys/gals make the finest leaders. ☐ ☐ ☐ ☐ ☐ Considerate people make the finest leaders.

6 Above all, leaders need to have objective reasoning.	☐	☐	☐	☐	☐	Above all, leaders need to be trusting and open.
7 Intelligent people make the better leaders.	☐	☐	☐	☐	☐	Experienced people make the better leaders.
8 Leadership is lonely.	☐	☐	☐	☐	☐	Leadership is gregarious.
9 Leaders keep a stiff upper lip about their feelings.	☐	☐	☐	☐	☐	Leaders let it all hang out, they say how they are feeling.
10 Leaders should be consistent.	☐	☐	☐	☐	☐	Leaders should adapt their style to suit.

Throughout the book you will find references to beliefs which may confirm or contradict what you believe. However, the point is not to test our agreement, but to extend *your thinking* about what leadership is for you.

What leadership means

Having a clear practical sense of what leadership means is a lot like knowing exactly where you are on a map. It is a dependable reference point for choosing a direction and taking decisions. And it is a signpost to where you might travel in your journey of personal discovery and development.

We all have our own ideas about what good leadership is and how we want to be led. Most people can vividly recall teachers, headmistresses, bosses and senior officers who were brilliant, lacklustre or just plain awful leaders. Perhaps the best place to start is with those memories.

Pause for thought

- On thinking about teachers, headmistresses, bosses and senior officers from your past, what did the brilliant ones do that made them so noteworthy?

- And what did the awful ones do to earn a downgrade in your memory?

- What approximately does 'leadership' mean for you right now?

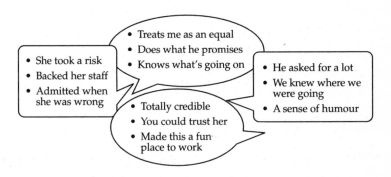

- Treats me as an equal
- Does what he promises
- Knows what's going on

- She took a risk
- Backed her staff
- Admitted when she was wrong

- He asked for a lot
- We knew where we were going
- A sense of humour

- Totally credible
- You could trust her
- Made this a fun place to work

Many interesting definitions can be found in the 20,000 or so studies and countless books written about leadership. Here are some of the main ones. Tick those that make sense to you.

Leadership is about:

- ☐ providing meaning and purpose
- ☐ focusing on the right things to do
- ☐ structuring the environment to achieve the organisation's goals
- ☐ getting others to do what you want
- ☐ motivating people to get things done willingly
- ☐ enabling others to take responsibility
- ☐ empowering others to do what they think is right
- ☐ helping people feel less fearful, more confident
- ☐ developing, sustaining and changing the culture
- ☐ having a bigger market share than competitors
- ☐ having the most prestigious products and services on the market.

Let's start with the most basic meaning. Most people agree that leadership is first and foremost about influencing. Leading is influencing people to get things done to a standard and quantity above their norm. And doing it willingly.

Leadership, therefore, is more than just having the authority of a supervisory or management position. Authority (or position power) gets you compliance. Influence gets you commitment. When you influence others to follow, they do so because they like you, admire you, stand in awe of you (referent power). Or because they believe you have special expertise to support their efforts (expert power).

Where leadership is found

The traditional theory is that all leaders are great men born with heroic talents. Caesar, Luther, Napoleon, Lincoln, Einstein, Churchill and other exalted figures.

The modern view is more realistic. First, women make great leaders too – Boadicea, Golda Meier, Margaret Thatcher, Marjorie Scardino (chief executive of the Pearson Group), to name but a few. Second, you do not have to be one of the great and the good. Leaders are found in every occupation and all ranks of society, many from humble origins. Jock Stein led Celtic to win the European Cup in 1967 – he started his working life as a coal miner. Mothers and fathers make great leaders. Third, many of the skills and qualities that make leaders effective are learned. The substantial investments in leadership training made by hard-headed captains of industry attest to that. However, most of the learning comes from experience.

'The top performers ask a further question: "What do I need to learn?" They don't waste time berating themselves for doing something badly. They look for shortfalls that impede their use of strengths, and for corrections ... From "What do I need to learn?" comes a variety of follow-ups. "What am I doing that I should do more of? That I should cut down? In what areas do I need to improve? What is the most effective way to get up to speed? Or can I delegate any of these areas to someone else?"' Charles Garfield

Leaders are everywhere

Traditional organisations often have relatively simple structures and operating processes. One or a very few leaders at the top make all the decisions. Other organisations are complex, dispersed and fast-moving. For them restricting leadership to the top echelons is neither feasible nor desirable. Leadership needs to be distributed to many people in all parts and levels of those enterprises.

Some companies in traditional manufacturing industries have improved their performance by recognising and reinforcing the leadership that goes on on the plant floor. In those progressive firms, 'empowerment' and 'self-managing teams' are more than buzz words.

'The leader builds dispersed and diverse leadership – distributing leadership to the outermost edges of the circle to unleash the power of shared responsibility.'
Frances Hesselbein

Leaders can be found throughout organisations of every sort – and not all in managing positions. This may cause confusion if you believe that all leaders are cut from the same cloth. In fact, they need to have different mind-sets and skills depending on where in the organisation they sit. In our distributed leadership model, every organisation requires three types of leadership: visionary, integration and fulfilment. You will find the symbols denoting these three types at various points in the book.

A model of leadership

	Leadership tasks	Leadership mind-set
Visionary leader e.g. director, senior executive, senior partner, chair and head of school, chancellor, senior dean	☐ Mission statement ☐ Vision, corporate values ☐ Anticipate, shape and respond to the external environment ☐ Transform the organisation ☐ Structure the organisation ☐ Please the shareholder ☐ Ensure organisational survival	☐ Long term ☐ Conceptual, big picture ☐ Externally oriented ☐ Broad interest in the industry ☐ Broad interest in the economy, regulation, politics
Integration leader e.g. department head, general manager of site/major plant, senior regional manager, junior partner	☐ Link units into the mission and vision ☐ Develop the organisation's system/process infrastructure ☐ Reconcile conflicting interests and goals between units ☐ Develop and champion a strong culture and leadership style ☐ Ensure the effective running of the whole organisation ☐ Innovate and use corporate knowledge ☐ Recruit and retain talent	☐ Medium term ☐ Boundary spanning ☐ Inside–outside orientation ☐ Facilitating ☐ Corporate values
Fulfilment leader e.g. senior teacher, project manager, shift supervisor, team leader, store manager, bank manager, audit manager/supervisor	☐ Please the customer/client ☐ Deliver operating results on time ☐ Make continuous improvements ☐ Unlock individual potential ☐ Increase productive use of resources ☐ Uphold the standards	☐ Short term ☐ Knowledge expert ☐ Results orientation ☐ Human psychology ☐ Customer service thinking ☐ Quality

The Distributed Leadership Model

Distributed leadership is about horses for courses – and courses for horses. Leaders at different levels have different mind-sets, different tasks to do. This means that leaders who excel in one level may not 'fit' at another level.

- *Good fit.* Jess a maintenance shift leader has come up through the ranks. Experienced and technically knowledgeable she is a completer–finisher. She is committed to providing her internal customers with an excellent maintenance service. And she runs a well-motivated team of fitters.
- *Poor fit.* Bernard is the manager in charge of production. While he lacks Jess's qualities, he has a talent for developing far-reaching visions of where the company should be. He has in-depth understanding of the market and where it is going. But those qualities are irrelevant to the leadership tasks he has to perform. We will meet him again in Chapter 5.

Far-sighted organisational leaders recognised the mismatch between task and talent. They put in place processes for identifying talent and matching it with the task requirements. The performance appraisal process is one way of doing it, but assessment centres are an even more useful way to discover hidden potential and match it to the task.

? Test Yourself

- Are you now operating more as a visionary, integration or fulfilment leader?
- Is that pretty much what your organisation requires of you right now?

- Which of the critical leadership tasks are yours?
- What is your mind-set(s) most of the time?
- Are there any new critical tasks or mind-sets you would like to explore or develop?

Don't stay inside the levels. Critical tasks and mind-sets may cut across types. 'Unlocking individual potential', for instance, may be an important task for leaders of any type. Make a note of your answers and any other thoughts prompted by the questions.

Building your own leadership model 1

- The one thing that strikes me as critically important about being a leader is ....
- What appeals to me most about being a leader is ....
- I see myself as a leader who ....
- The type of distributed leader that I am best equipped to be is ....
- The type of distributed leader that I would very much like to be is ....

The right stuff – what you bring to the party

Self-knowledge

Leaders who really know themselves have the inside track. They play to their strengths. They structure their jobs and organise the work to make their weaknesses less relevant and less visible. They know when to lead and when to stand back. They know when to involve others who have the talents they lack. They know when to seek advice. And they know what they need to develop in themselves.

This chapter will enable you to identify:

- your strong leadership qualities, the ones you will keep on playing to
- the qualities you will develop and expand
- the self-image you mean to have as your ideal.

The right stuff

What is the 'right stuff' for being a leader?

? **Test Yourself**

- What do you think are the three most important qualities a leader ought to have?
- If you had to pick just one, what would it be? Why that one?

People seldom come up with the same answers. If your answer is 'it depends', that is exactly what our model would say. It depends on the challenges, the situation, who else is involved. Experts often disagree about qualities of leadership because they are talking about different types of leadership. Our Distributed Leadership Model is a good starting point for examining the qualities of different types.

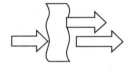

• The fulfilment qualities are the right stuff leaders require to initiate action, influence others to make it happen, and deliver results to a required high standard. These qualities come close to being the universal requirements for leaders.

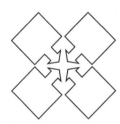

• Next come the integration qualities, which are vitally important in complex and turbulent environments. Where the present is confusing and the future uncertain. Where people have conflicting goals and diverse backgrounds. Where there is a lot of anxiety and insecurity. Where change is needed but resistance is high.

• The final list of qualities is associated with what President Reagan famously called 'the vision thing'. Groups and organisations are all part of a larger social, political and economic system. A fundamental task of the leader is to secure an advantageous place in the system for the group or organisation. And to influence events in the larger system to their benefit. This means having a broader boundary-spanning perspective. And it means having a longer time horizon than the people he or she leads. These are the visionary qualities.

?

Test Yourself
Self-assessment key

Rate yourself		
☺ outstanding	☻ average	☹ mmm-h

Action plan		
👍 Keep on doing	∅ Discuss with a friend	🍸 Strengthen it

Assessing your fulfilment qualities

	Rate yourself ☺ ☻ ☹	Action plan 👍 ∅ 🍸
1 **Self-confidence**. Self-assured, you believe in yourself and your ability to achieve your goals.	☐ ☐ ☐	☐ ☐ ☐
2 **Self-control**. Under pressure and provocation you are usually able to give a rational, well-balanced response.	☐ ☐ ☐	☐ ☐ ☐
3 **Integrity**. Being honest, consistent and doing the right thing are important to you.	☐ ☐ ☐	☐ ☐ ☐
4 **Positive outlook**. You are positive and upbeat, though realistic and practical as well.	☐ ☐ ☐	☐ ☐ ☐
5 **Personal impact**. You project a positive image of yourself – through your grooming, clothes, manner, voice.	☐ ☐ ☐	☐ ☐ ☐

	Rate yourself			Action plan		
	☺	😐	☹	👍	∅	🏋
6 Power drive. You are motivated to influence people and events, to make things happen through others.	☐	☐	☐	☐	☐	☐
7 Achievement orientation. You have high standards, want to do things better, and keep measuring your effectiveness.	☐	☐	☐	☐	☐	☐
8 Follow-through. Completing the task, getting the result is one of your drivers.	☐	☐	☐	☐	☐	☐
9 Critical reasoning. You can see the wood for the trees, analyse the whole into parts, and grasp causes and effects.	☐	☐	☐	☐	☐	☐
10 Focus. You evaluate priorities, continually concentrating attention and effort on the goals that matter the most.	☐	☐	☐	☐	☐	☐
11 Speaking. You can get your ideas and arguments across and create the impression you want to create.	☐	☐	☐	☐	☐	☐

	Rate yourself			Action plan		
	☺	😐	☹	👍	∅	🏆
12 Active listening. You are understanding and responsive to others' ideas, feelings and thinking.	☐	☐	☐	☐	☐	☐
13 Influencing. You are able to bring others along with you, to win and maintain their commitment.	☐	☐	☐	☐	☐	☐
14 Teambuilding. You know how to develop, motivate and maintain effective teams.	☐	☐	☐	☐	☐	☐
15 Insider understanding. You have a sound understanding of the goals and thinking of your organisation.	☐	☐	☐	☐	☐	☐

Good leaders score average or higher on the fulfilment qualities. But nobody is outstanding in all of them, not even 'great men' – or great women. Six or more 'outstandings' is about as good as it gets. Think of incidents in your life that brought your 'outstandings' to the fore. Plan how to do more of the same.

?

Test Yourself
Assessing your integration qualities

	Rate yourself ☺ ☺ ☹	Action plan 👍 Ø Ⴘ
1 Energy. You are well able to cope with prolonged periods of intense effort when high-quality output is required.	☐ ☐ ☐	☐ ☐ ☐
2 Tolerance of uncertainty. You accept ambiguity and maintain effectiveness when information, goal and course of action are uncertain or unclear.	☐ ☐ ☐	☐ ☐ ☐
3 Structuring. You are good at detecting links between isolated events, and bringing order and shape out of confusion.	☐ ☐ ☐	☐ ☐ ☐
4 Conceptual thinking. You can see patterns, trends and discontinuities; you formulate ideas that make sense of confusing problems; and you draw sound conclusions from data.	☐ ☐ ☐	☐ ☐ ☐

	Rate yourself ☺ ☐ ☹	Action plan 👍 ∅ ⅄
5 Balanced judgement. When making decisions you can balance hard facts and soft feelings, the heart and the head.	☐ ☐ ☐	☐ ☐ ☐
6 Values-based thinking. You believe in the importance of trust, openness and other values to individuals and to organisations.	☐ ☐ ☐	☐ ☐ ☐
7 Communication tactics. You understand how to use different kinds of communication in different situations and for different purposes and people.	☐ ☐ ☐	☐ ☐ ☐
8 Networking. You know how to develop and maintain networks inside and outside the organisation, and how to use your contacts to support your goals.	☐ ☐ ☐	☐ ☐ ☐
9 Political savvy. You understand and are able to manage the power relationships, vested interests and coalitions.	☐ ☐ ☐	☐ ☐ ☐

	Rate yourself ☺ ☺ ☹	Action plan 👍 ∅ 🏆
10 Change management ability. You understand and can manoeuvre the levers of change. You are skilled in initiating, mobilising, implementing and bringing about change.	☐ ☐ ☐	☐ ☐ ☐
11 Industry knowledge. You know your industry, its products, services, markets and customers, the competitors and contenders, the trends and developments.	☐ ☐ ☐	☐ ☐ ☐

When you are totting up your self-assessments the same advice applies: no one is outstanding in all the qualities.

Use these qualities to assess your development needs if you aspire to move from fulfilment to integration leadership. The higher your aim, the more demanding your standard of assessment should be. For example, what would be judged as strong conceptual thinking in fulfilment leadership will probably be considered average in integration leadership.

?

Test Yourself
Assessing your visionary qualities

	Rate yourself ☺ ☻ ☹	Action plan 👍 ∅ 🏋

1 **Scope of thinking**. You have a wide, longer term perspective and a range of knowledge and ideas that enable you to grasp the big picture in the external environment.

☐ ☐ ☐ | ☐ ☐ ☐

2 **Visionary thinking**. You can develop a vision for your team or organisation's future that is inspiring but practical, challenging but attainable.

☐ ☐ ☐ | ☐ ☐ ☐

3 **Cognitive complexity.** You think in multiple dimensions, and solutions. You see hidden relationships in messy, complex situations. You adapt your ideas and views to new concepts and evidence.

☐ ☐ ☐ | ☐ ☐ ☐

4 **Uncertainty balance.** You balance planning with adapting, the need for control with the need for flexibility.

☐ ☐ ☐ | ☐ ☐ ☐

	Rate yourself			Action plan		
	☺	😐	☹	👍	∅	Υ
5 Spokesperson. You are a passionate champion of the team or organisation to the external world.	☐	☐	☐	☐	☐	☐
6 Organisational know-how. You have expert understanding of the inner workings, structures, funding, processes and roles of organisations and teams.	☐	☐	☐	☐	☐	☐
7 Cultural know-how. You understand the culture(s) within which the organisation operates and has its markets.	☐	☐	☐	☐	☐	☐
8 Political know-how. You understand the political, statutory and regulatory environment affecting the industry, its markets and your business.	☐	☐	☐	☐	☐	☐
9 Economic impacts. You have an informed economic view. You understand economic forecasts, indicators and trends as they might affect business, the industry and its markets.	☐	☐	☐	☐	☐	☐

	Rate yourself	Action plan
	☺ ☻ ☹	👍 ∅ 🏆
10 Social and demographic impacts. You understand the issues, attitudes and distribution of groups in society as they might affect business, the industry and its markets.	☐ ☐ ☐	☐ ☐ ☐

Again be advised: no one is outstanding in all of the visionary qualities. Note also that you may have some visionary qualities, which can put to good use, even though your role is not a visionary role. 'Visionary thinking', for example. Every team, every organisation needs a vision to follow. Look for opportunities on task forces or in projects where you can apply your visionary qualities to the work of your organisation.

> 'The capacity to paint an uplifting and ennobling picture of the future is, in fact, what differentiates leaders from other credible sources.' Kouzes and Posner

Nigel is a senior area manager for one of the UK high-street banks. He is conscientious about 'getting on with the work'. Vision, he believes, isn't his job. It is done by the top executives of the bank. Trouble is, they didn't do it either. This leaves Nigel and the tellers, clerks and branch managers with no idea where they are supposed to be headed.

Pause for thought

• Looking back on your self-assessment, would others who know you have rated you the same? Why not ask them?

Task- or relationship-oriented?

A vast body of research has identified task-structure and human-relations orientations as major dimensions of leadership. Task-oriented leaders focus mostly on structuring the task, production and getting the job done. Relationship-oriented leaders are more concerned with people and supporting them.

? **Test Yourself**

Think of the person at work with whom you could work *least* well. Rate him or her on the following dimensions by circling the appropriate number. Then add up the numbers you circled.

The least preferred co-worker scale

rejecting	1	2	3	4	5	6	7	8	accepting
supportive	8	7	6	5	4	3	2	1	hostile
distant	1	2	3	4	5	6	7	8	close
pleasant	8	7	6	5	4	3	2	1	unpleasant
open	8	7	6	5	4	3	2	1	guarded
friendly	8	7	6	5	4	3	2	1	unfriendly
untrustworthy	1	2	3	4	5	6	7	8	trustworthy
inefficient	1	2	3	4	5	6	7	8	efficient
self-assured	8	7	6	5	4	3	2	1	hesitant
boring	1	2	3	4	5	6	7	8	interesting

A score of 40 or higher means that you are more relationship-oriented. You place premium in being considerate to your followers. A score of 35 or lower means you are more task-controlling and less concerned with the human relations aspect. The more extreme your scores, up or down, the more likely you are to act out your predominant style.

You may argue that it is possible for you to be high in both task and people orientations. That is quite true. Or you might be low in both, or a bit of a mixture. In short, you can be in any one of four leadership style quadrants:

High human-relations orientation	**Consideration** Friendly and responsive, you treat the individual as a whole person and create a spirit of good will	**Collaborating** You involve and cooperate with those above, below and horizontally to achieve shared goals
	Laissez faire You give staff scope to do their own thing while you get on with doing yours	**Directing** You operate in telling mode and are very clear about what needs doing, by when
Low human-relations orientation	Low task-structure orientation	High task-structure orientation

Leadership style quadrants

? Test Yourself

- In which quadrant would you place yourself? Would those who know you well agree?
- Experts disagree about how much you can adapt your style to what the situation demands. How competent would you be in moving from quadrant to quadrant as the demands of the situation change?

Assessing your images of leadership

When you 'do' leadership over a period of time you acquire your own unique style. You evolve your own 'rules' about how to lead – beliefs you live by, principles you apply, preferred ways of handling people and situations. These coalesce into the image you have of yourself as a leader. You usually take the image for granted without giving it much thought.

Becoming fully aware of the image gives you a deeper understanding of why and how you are effective or ineffective. You can keep repeating the styles and behaviours you know are successful. Equally, becoming aware gives you insight into what is switching people off. And you can then change or improve.

'Images of Leadership' is a model created to help leaders develop successful approaches. It contains five different images or patterns of leadership: Expert, Driver, Friend, Hero and Guide.

? Test Yourself

Take a few minutes to assess your 'Images of Leadership'. You have 100 points in total to assign to the five images. Assign the points to show how big a part each image plays in your leadership style.

The Expert

- I take pride in my technical/professional mastery.
- I enjoy applying my expertise to challenging projects.
- I like going around bureaucracy to get things done.
- I tend to tackle the complex technical issues myself.
- I focus on the task more than the people, paying less attention to their development.
- I take little notice of the wider corporate picture.

The Driver

- I am known as tough-minded and demanding but also fair and supportive.
- I give people clear direction and instruction.
- I schedule the work to be done.
- I pride myself on following through, getting the details right.
- I closely monitor and measure performance.
- I encourage the use of uniform procedures.

The Friend

- I like to be liked.
- I am known to be friendly and approachable.
- I make a point of giving recognition and showing respect.
- I treat members of the group as my equals.

- I strive continually to create a spirit of goodwill.
- I do personal favours for the group.

The Hero

- I command the centre stage and set the agenda.
- People know me as a strong leader in times of crisis.
- I have a reputation for being competitive and assertive.
- I set challenging targets and require people to deliver them.
- I manoeuvre the levers of power with practised ease and confidence.
- I tend to eclipse others.

The Guide

- I put the wider corporate goals before narrow self-interest.
- I have a reputation for being a strong communicator and facilitator.
- I am really committed to developing a positive, cooperative culture.
- I strive to develop a high-performance team(s).
- Bringing out the best in people is an essential part of my make-up.
- I have little patience with organisation politics.

- Now ask someone who knows you well – colleague, mentor or someone in your team – to assess your leadership images. Go off and think about what they say. Then come back and discuss their impressions.

Here is the leadership image of Pete who is a senior marketing manager.

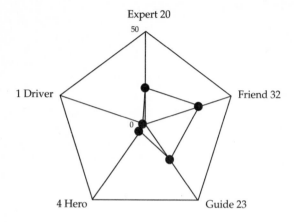

Images of leadership profile

Pete has an MBA, is intelligent and is highly professional in his role. Being an extremely agreeable person he tends to get on well with almost everyone, particularly the members of his team. They appreciate his gentle approach and what he does for their development. He has enjoyed managing things pretty much as he liked and was happy in the job until the company underwent a restructuring. He is now expected to work hand-in-hand with his colleague, the operations manager, who is a bit of a Hero. Their boss Linda is a bullying type. Pete does not cope very well with the politics and power plays. You can see that his images are out of kilter with the new reality. We will return to Pete in Chapters 4 and 5.

The five images can be mapped onto the task and people leadership quadrants. The Friend is very high on human relations, very low on task structure. The Hero is the opposite: low on human relations and high on task.

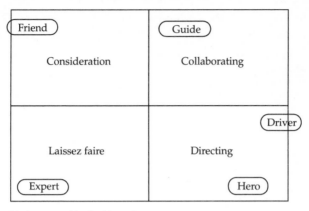

Friend	Guide
Consideration	Collaborating
	Driver
Laissez faire	Directing
Expert	Hero

Leadership images and leadership styles

No one image is intrinsically better than another. Each has advantages and blind spots. But having a balance between task styles (Expert, Driver, Hero) and people styles (Friend, Guide) is better than being all one level or all the other. Balanced styles give you added flexibility.

Building your own leadership model 2

- Would you change your 'three most important qualities a leader should have?' To what?
- What are your strengths? Any you underestimate?
- Is your dominant self-image the style you want to be?
- Is there a balance between your task style (Expert, Driver or Hero) and your people style (Friend or Guide)?

- What are the qualities and styles that give you potential for higher levels of leadership?
- What are the gaps between the qualities and styles you have and those you want to have? How do you think you will close the gaps?
- How closely do your self-assessments match the feedback you get from others?

Take people with you – winning commitment

The 'Listen, sunshine' school of management

At one time or another many of us have been on the receiving end of the 'listen, sunshine' school of management. Bullying, is another word for it. Bullying which drains motivation and commitment. If you want more from people than grudging compliance, you need to win their hearts and minds.

To do that you need to understand:

- what power is and how to use it wisely
- how to give individuals different strokes
- what makes people different
- what people yearn for.

You really need to want to

If there is one single attribute quality that is essential to being a leader it is, above all, *the will to lead*. You need to want to lead others. And you need to be able to use influence. The psychologist David McClelland was one of the most significant thinkers on the subject of managers' motivation and competence. His research has shown that managers with high power needs are the most successful. Morale, team spirit and sales are higher under high-power leaders than leaders who are friendly and agreeable.

'I would rather be first in a small village in Gaul than second in command in Rome.' Julius Caesar

Wanting power is not the same as being autocratic or being motivated by self-interest. The really effective leaders wield power in the interests of their institutions and their followers. And powerful leaders often have democratic, coaching styles.

> 'Successful managers – what we called institutional managers – have a strong need for power (that is, for influencing others) that is greater than the need to be liked, and they exhibit self-control.' David McClelland

The need for achievement is also important. Achievement drive is monitoring performance and striving for improvements and efficiencies. Understandably, the success of a *small* company owes more to the leader's need for achievement than need for power.

The levers of power

Influence means exercising power. Leaders can leverage different kinds of power.

- *Reward power*. Being able to give or withhold incentives. Rewards may be tangible (time off, a preferred assignment, promotion, pay rise) or intangible (praise, attention, recognition). Often associated with organisational position, the base of reward power is usually compliance.
- *Coercive power*. Control over sanctions, which may also be tangible (suspension, formal reprimand, undesirable assignment) or intangible (disapproval, social exclusion).

The power base is fear. It is often derived from organisational position.

- *Legitimate power*. Based on recognised organisational authority, legitimate power usually flows from a formal position (position power) and the social distance between the leader and the led. Official documents are a source of legitimate power. The base is usually compliance.
- *Referent power*. Influence based on liking, friendship, admiration or personal loyalty. This usually develops slowly in a one-to-one relationship of consideration and respect. Leaders create referent power by encouraging participation and by championing the interests of their staff. Those led come to identify with the leader.
- *Expert power*. Influence based on the followers' belief in the leader's superior knowledge and expertise, real or imagined. The expert leader is seen as a credible source of information and advice.

From a humanistic perspective, referent and expert power seem to be preferable to the other sources. From a practical perspective, they promise a more enduring bond between leader and led. But in fact all sources can be appropriate depending on the situation and context. When the going gets rough, successful leaders play hardball to good effect.

Dominance versus commitment

How you wield power depends a lot on whether you intend to dominate or gain commitment. Any or all of the power levers can be used to dominate (Hitler) or to build commitment (Martin Luther King). Your choice. Here is how it works.

You establish dominance by:

- putting people down
- centralising control
- manipulating rewards and punishment
- withholding information
- using public relations to manipulate opinion
- developing a cult of personality dedicated to you
- increasing your followers' dependence on you their leader

- building people up
- exercising and delegating authority in a responsible way
- sharing information
- encouraging participation in decisions
- building followers' skills and self-confidence
- building commitment to the organisation and its values
- giving a positive example
- encouraging your followers to be independent

You develop commitment by:

Dominance versus commitment

? | ## Test Yourself

- Thinking of particular incidents in the last few months, tick the first column if you used a power lever to influence people.
- Tick any levers of power you tend to use a lot.
- When you use a lever, does it tend to fall under dominance (Dom) or commitment (Com)?
- Do you think those on the receiving end felt positive (+) or negative (−)?
- Are your chances of taking them with you high or low?

Power lever	Have used	Use often	Feels right	Dom or	Com	+ or	−	High or Low
Reward	☐	☐	☐	☐	☐	☐	☐	☐
Coercive	☐	☐	☐	☐	☐	☐	☐	☐
Legitimate	☐	☐	☐	☐	☐	☐	☐	☐
Referent	☐	☐	☐	☐	☐	☐	☐	☐
Expert	☐	☐	☐	☐	☐	☐	☐	☐

Different strokes for different folks

It is the small things that count.

Duncan tells the story of when as a young lieutenant he saw his first action with the Royal Marines against the Mau Mau independence movement of Kenya. When resting his men at the water holes he made a habit of filling their canteens and handing them out before resuming patrol. Gradually this habit lapsed as his experience grew and prospects of promotion occupied his attention. Then one day back at base Sergeant Archer 'took me behind the bike shed'. 'Sir,' said the sergeant, 'You remember when you used to fill our bottles on patrol? The lads respected you for that, even when they got the wrong bottles. You don't give a toss for them now and that is about how they feel about you.' 'I never regained my credibility after that', said Duncan ruefully, 'but what a lesson learned.'

Strokes are the currency leaders use to exercise influence. Stroking means giving a person your attention – acknowledging that they exist. Filling their water bottles. A pat on the back. Chatting about how the kids are doing at school. Cracking a joke. A reprimand or pointedly ignoring someone are negative strokes.

Because people are different, giving everyone the same strokes makes no sense at all. Stroke *tokens* have different value for different people. What is a stroke for one may not be for another. Liz perceives a squeeze of the arm as a sign of appreciation. Jean sees it as a patronising gesture. Beth sees it as sexual harassment. It is absolutely essential for leaders to understand this and to pay in the right coin.

The amount of stroking that individuals hunger for varies widely. Some have huge appetites. In stroke deficit they do almost anything – favourable or unfavourable – to get attention. Dan hanging around your office on a pretext. Jean claiming credit for something she didn't write. Edmund staying behind 'to do extra work'. All signals saying 'I need to be stroked.' Or perhaps, I need to have a talk about what is bothering me.

Other individuals are the opposite. Having received little of it in the past, John is uncomfortable with positive stroking now. Sensitive leaders don't give up. They continue to give quiet encouragement for good performance, until individuals like John eventually come to appreciate themselves and to appreciate being appreciated. If you are a bit like that yourself, practice accepting positive strokes gracefully. It works. And it is also a positive stroke to the stroker. The reverse – accepting a positive stroke with bad grace – is a putdown.

Different groups and organisations have different *stroke economies*. Some have a *positive stroke economy* (encouraging, recognising, being solution-oriented, having fun). Others have a negative one (blaming, criticising, sarcasm, arguing). The first kind brings out the best in people and grows their commitment. A *negative stroke economy* brings out the worst and grows submission and compliance. It is the difference between catching people doing something right and catching them doing something wrong.

> *'Catch people doing something right.'*
> *Slogan used in the cultural transformation of British*
> *Airways in the 1980s*

Trading jokes was the way one team gave each other strokes. Lindy had the best and her jokes became the traditional start to business meetings. Promoted to head up a bigger department she took the joke tradition with her. And so it was she opened her very first meeting with the immortal words 'Did you hear the one about ...'. Silence. Not a word spoken. After much clearing of throats the meeting got back on a sober course. It took Lindy months to live down her reputation as 'the lightweight who can't take business seriously'.

To know what strokes to give you need to know what makes people different.

What makes people different

No two people have the same personality or motivation structure. Not even twins. Even when you are leading a team you are leading individuals. When you understand and treat each member of the team as a unique person, then you know how to motivate the team.

Some of the more interesting ways in which people differ are described in the Myers–Briggs Type Indicator, a psychological model.

? Test Yourself

- Think once again of the person at work with whom you could work *least* well.
- Rate him/her as more to the right or more to the left on each pair of Myers–Briggs preferences.
- Now rate your own preferences on the Myers–Briggs scales.
- What are the most striking differences and similarities between your preferences and your co-worker's?
- Now that you understand how he/she and you are different, what might you do to win that person's commitment?

Very clear		No preference			Very clear	
☐	☐	☐	☐	☐	☐	☐

Extraverts are outgoing. Get a buzz from action, people, things happening. They speak out before thinking what they want to say.

Introverts are quiet and reserved. They enjoy their own company. They enjoy mulling things over before speaking out.

☐   ☐   ☐   ☐   ☐   ☐   ☐

Sensing. Sensors are most at ease with facts. They prefer working with today's realities. Practical and good with detail.

Intuition. Intuitives are oriented towards future possibilities; they revel in ideas, theories and what could be.

☐   ☐   ☐   ☐   ☐   ☐   ☐

Rational thinking. They prefer logical analysis, making choices and decisions based on rational cause-and-effect. Objective.

Feeling. They focus on what is important personally to them and to others. Identify with feelings and values. Subjective.

☐   ☐   ☐   ☐   ☐   ☐   ☐

Judging. They prefer to live in a planned, orderly way, regulating and controlling their lives and have things settled.

Perceiving. They prefer to live in a flexible, spontaneous way; relishing experience and keeping the options open.

The Myers–Briggs Model

Here are clues about what brings out the best in people with different psychological preferences.

The Myers–Briggs work preferences

Extraverting
- Variety, having several assignments to work on
- Action, springing into action, a change of pace
- Opportunities to work, talk, interact with others
- Brainstorming with others
- Learning through action and discussion

Introverting
- Concentrating on one project at a time
- A quiet, private work setting
- Quality thinking time – free from interruption
- Communicating one-on-one or in writing
- Time to express themselves at their own pace

Sensing
- Getting the job detail first, then the bigger picture
- Practical work fixing today's problems
- Using practised routines and skills
- Having the steps of a process/task spelled out
- Working with and praise for attention to detail

Intuition
- Seeing the job in the round first, then the specifics
- Developing possibilities and plans for the future
- Exploring creative ideas, trying novel ways
- Learning new skills for the challenge and novelty
- Talking in bold outline without the 'trivial' details

Thinking

- Justice – being treated fairly and equitably
- Working with problems that can be analysed objectively and impartially
- Debating issues logically and unemotionally
- Managing and dealing objectively with people
- Using principles/truths as the basis for decisions

Feeling

- Work requiring concern for people and their interests
- A harmonious working environment
- Recognition in debate of their feelings and values
- Paying attention to others' likes and dislikes
- Counselling and helping others

Judging

- Working in a planned and structured way
- Making decisions quickly, moving things forward
- Limiting facts and options, simplifying decisions
- Being prepared, avoiding last-minute stresses
- Learning what one needs for the task at hand

Perceiving

- Working in a flexible fast-changing environment
- Being able to consider all the facts and options
- Postponing current tasks to meet momentary needs
- Not being restricted by plans and deadlines
- Learning lots of interesting things

Tests like the Myers–Briggs Type Indicator give leaders a useful psychological vocabulary for understanding and relating to individuals and teams. Psychometric tests are widely used in many countries to measure these and other interesting differences.

What people yearn for

People in organisations have self-evident 'hygiene' needs – for safety and security, pay, comfort facilities and physical safety. They need to know what their duties are and the standards that are expected. They need to be trained and coached. They need feedback. They need to be recognised and rewarded and disciplined. They need to have opportunities for advancement. In well-managed organisations the practices, systems and procedures for meeting these expectations have become routine. They are the basics that managers deliver.

But people in their hearts and minds yearn for much more:

?

Test Yourself

- Tick the yearnings felt by the people you work with. If you don't know, how can you find out?
- Tick those that you yourself feel.
- Pick just one of these yearnings that you could do much more to help others fulfil in themselves.
- How do you propose to do that?

		People at work	Me	Will do more
1	To be treated fairly and equitably	☐	☐	☐
2	To belong, to be accepted	☐	☐	☐
3	To be respected, to have influence	☐	☐	☐
4	To be liked and appreciated	☐	☐	☐

		People at work	Me	Will do more
5	To enjoy work and to be happy when going about it	☐	☐	☐
6	To have harmonious relationships	☐	☐	☐
7	To be effective and successful	☐	☐	☐
8	To satisfy their own personal interests – the 'what's in it for me' factor.	☐	☐	☐

These are what make work worthwhile and not just a job. Serving these needs is arguably the most important task the leader has.

You can easily tell when these yearnings are being neglected. You hear people saying:

- 'Management has double standards, one rule for us, one rule for them.'
- 'I don't think management trusts us to do the job.'
- 'Management treats people like dirt. They can't be trusted. I am here to sponge off this company as much as I can until I find a new job.'
- 'Mistrust between employees on the factory floor leads to a lot of arguments and tension.'
- 'We now have a fear culture where it is more important to blame someone than to find a solution.'
- 'We flog dead horses and do things a certain way because that's how we have always done them.'
- 'You don't get 100% commitment from your staff if you treat them like mushrooms.'
- 'Senior-level politics make the simplest solutions impossible.'

Sound familiar?

> *'The ideal leader, therefore, cannot be merely successful. He must bring out the best in people.'*
> *Michael Maccoby*

Here are some of the things that good leaders do to give people meaning:

- *Honesty and openness*. They give trust and they earn trust. They say what they mean and mean what they say. No fudging, no economy with the truth. They trust people with their confidences. They explain when there are things they cannot disclose.
- *Respect*. They help people feel important. They give them quality time. They explain and discuss the strategy and what is happening in the business. They genuinely seek people's inputs and ideas. They treat people with good manners.
- *Including*. They make the individual feel one of the team. They welcome them every day. They give news to their followers first before any outsiders. They invite them to important meetings and events. They take an active part in away days and social events.
- *Justice*. Leaders do not play favourites. They give people confidence that rewards and compensation will be distributed fairly. When the UK Treasury imposed pay restraints on public servants, prime minister Tony Blair refused to take the substantial pay increase he was entitled to.
- *Equality*. Leaders do away with the executive dining room and other status barriers. They give plant floor staff

the same rights and privileges as the office staff. At British Airways, Colin Marshal, the CEO, insisted that *everyone* wore their first name on their lapel. They champion diversity in the workforce.

- *Pride in the enterprise*. By communicating vision and meaning, leaders give individuals pride in their work. The floor-sweeper at NASA took enormous pride in his work because he was 'helping to put a man on the moon'.

- *Fun and excitement*. Anne is a regional president in one of the global credit card associations. For the Scotland *v* Brazil 1998 World Cup match, she laid on a giant TV screen, drinks and snacks. Employees were able to enjoy the game and make up the time at their discretion

These are the reasons for building strong values in your organisation.

'A strong organizational culture is capable of inspiring high levels of commitment and truly inspired behavior ... employees can be attracted to a set of beliefs and values that can inspire a broad commitment to organizational performance. Such commitment, however, is much more difficult to get than simple compliance. It is also difficult to sustain over time, but can produce extraordinary results.'
Leonard A. Schlesinger and Richard J. Balzer

'Sunshine management' or commitment leadership?

This chapter has posed a basic choice: 'sunshine management' or commitment leadership? 'The monster upstairs who's unapproachable?' or the leader of whom people say, 'I really could work for her/him.' It isn't just a matter of your personal values – though that is important too. In the long term, it is a matter of what is best for the enterprise. Committed people deliver better quality, better products and services, better productivity and a better future than conscripts ever could.

Building your own leadership model 3

- Which do you choose – 'sunshine' management or commitment leadership?
- How are you going to use power? To what end?
- Do you fill water bottles or pursue your own ambitions?
- What strokes will you give, what stroke economy will you develop?
- Of the several or many people that you could influence, what do they yearn for? How can you serve them better?

The right place, the right time

Choosing your ground

Ronald Reagan, the B-movie actor, became President Reagan, leader of the world's most powerful democracy. Weak on detail and short on analysis, he had one overriding quality. He was 'the great communicator' at a time when mass communication through television had become the key to success at the voting polls. He was in the right place at the right time.

In 1991, Russia's Boris Yeltsin played second fiddle to the Soviet leader Michail Gorbachev. But one day in August saw a reversal in their fortunes. While Mr Gorbachev vacationed at the Black Sea, Mr Yeltsin was in the streets of Moscow outfacing Communist Party hardliners – and riding to supreme power on the back of a tank. Arguably, Yeltsin had more of the right stuff for the times – ruthlessness, a flair for the dramatic and popular charisma. And he too was in the right place at the right time.

To survive and succeed as a leader means having the right stuff for the place and the time. This chapter is about finding that fit. It has four topics:

- Mapping out the opportunities and threats
- Navigating the political minefields
- Surviving difficult colleagues
- Being objective about yourself.

Mapping out the opportunities and threats

What kind of organisation and what sort of environment
allow you to kick with your best foot? Some leaders come
into their own in small start-up businesses, others in large
blue-chip companies. Some excel in boom times, others
when it is time to batten down the hatches.

Bob was the larger-than-life Chief Executive of a rambling
construction group. As long as the economy boomed and
property values escalated, he was brilliantly successful.
When the downturn inevitably came, Bob was totally
wanting in initiative, and his most constructive act was to
resign. Anthony, his brusque and introverted successor,
presided over the group's liquidation. With feet firmly
planted in reality and a canny head for cash flow, Anthony
successfully salvaged parts of the group, found funds to meet
the last payroll, and set up a job centre for the employees.

Different styles of leadership are also required at different
stages in an organisation's life cycle.

The life cycle of an organisation
Over its life, an organisation typically goes through a cycle
of growth, levelling off and then declining. In the decline
stage, there are three options: wind up of the business,
takeover by another firm, or radical transformation and
renewal.

Each stage and each option require quite different styles of
strategic thinking. At the start-up and when radical change
is needed to avoid decay, *innovative thinking* is essential. At
other times, *adaptive thinking* is required to underpin the
business with efficient and effective processes. But adapting

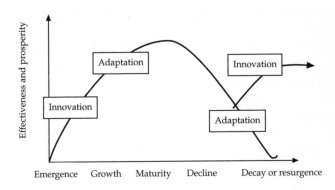

The life cycle stages

when the firm is in terminal decline is like rearranging the deckchairs on the Titanic.

In fact, any organisation needs to have the capability to innovate and adapt, with each style dominating the other as circumstances change.

In the 1980s, British Airways was going through a radical transformation – from arthritic publicly owned bureaucracy to flexible market-driven business. A high-flier programme was launched to select and develop the leaders of the future. Research into what distinguished those with the strongest leadership potential pointed clearly to the tendency to think innovatively. At that time in the life cycle, entrepreneurial innovative thinking was at a premium. In the late 1990s, the balance shifted to favour adaptation – working within the box, increasing efficiencies and taking out the costs. Interestingly, that was the time when the old, sober coat of arms and the Union Jack were restored, replacing the bright, creative but short-lived artwork on the tail fins.

The innovation–adaptation thinking styles have been researched and measured by the English psychologist Michael Kirton. He found that individuals are naturally innovative or adaptive in their thinking. Or else they are 'bridgers' with a mental foot in both styles.

? ## Test Yourself

- Where on the adaptation–innovation scale would you place your thinking style?
- How well does your thinking style fit with the organisation's life cycle?
- What are the advantages and disadvantages for you?
- Where do you think you can find the best fit for your style?

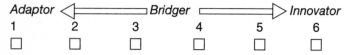

Adaptor			*Bridger*		*Innovator*
1	2	3	4	5	6
☐	☐	☐	☐	☐	☐

- Thinking inside the box
- Oriented towards stability
- Improving the existing system
- Using well-tried thinking
- Conforming to the rules

- Thinking outside the box
- Questioning basic assumptions
- Challenging the consensus
- Oriented towards change
- Doing things differently

The style and culture fit

Progressive organisations go to great lengths to recruit the right people. They invest in psychometric testing, assessment centres and other assessment provisions. Yet, at the end of the day, their instincts take over and the jobs go to 'people like us'. People who will fit in with 'the way we do things around here' – that is, the organisation's norms and culture.

Every organisation has its own cultural style that exerts a powerful influence on people's perceptions and behaviour. Leaders are both creators of that style and followers of its unwritten rules. Where the cultural norm is to tell and direct, leaders in the Driver mold (see Chapter 2) fit in very well. They also fit when followers are low in ability or where tasks are unstructured or unfamiliar. Hero fits most comfortably in a power culture, while the Friend style works well in agreeable cultures where harmony is the norm.

However, a leader's style may run against the cultural mainstream. Elsewhere, the style may be acceptable, but here it goes against the cultural grain. It causes friction that diverts people's attention from their task. This happens, for example, when Heroes find themselves in agreeable, considerate cultures. Where the tasks are familiar and well within people's ability, Drivers will be seen as meddling and Heroes as patronising.

Leader mismatches often occur for no reason other than 'that's just the way I am'. It is quite a different matter from when a leader is deliberately modeling and encouraging an opposite style to change the prevailing norm.

Everyone – leaders included – makes concessions and bends their behaviour and style to group norms and culture. But too much concession of one's preferred style causes strain. The more incompatible the mix, the greater the strain and frustration on both sides. If required to conform too far or for too long to an incompatible norm, leaders will tend to snap back to their dominant preferred style of leading.

Friend	Guide
Considerate culture	Collaborative culture
	Driver
Expert	Directing culture
Laissez faire culture	Hero

Hero	Expert
Considerate culture	Collaborative culture
Driver	
Laissez faire culture	Directing culture
Guide	Friend

Compatible combinations of leadership styles and organisation cultures

Incompatible combinations of leadership styles and organisation cultures

James, a strong Hero, left his blue-chip company to build a management consulting business. His plan was to win and lead prestigious government projects, calling in independent associates as required. For a time he was able to play the Friend and Expert roles with the associates. But invariably James's Hero would emerge, play power games, and alienate his associates. As the pattern kept on repeating itself James's supply of associates ran out. He now works with inexperienced followers who are content to be told what to do.

Moral: find a culture in which your preferred style flourishes, or find a role where style matters little. The alternative – barring a personality transplant – is a lengthy course of personal development.

To assess your fit with the culture, evaluate your own preferred ways, the ways of the organisation, and the gap between the two.

? Test Yourself

- Rate the culture of your organisation on a scale where 1 means 'not at all like the culture' and 10 means 'exactly like the culture'.
- Rate your own personal preferences on a 1-to-10 scale: 1 means 'this is not at all what I like or want' and 10 means 'this is exactly what I like and want'.
- Subtract your style scores from the culture scores to find the difference – the gap.
- What does the pattern of similarities and differences say about your organisational fit?

	The culture	*You*	*The gap*
1 *Considerate* – be friendly, be supportive, please others.	☐	☐	☐
2 *Collaborative* – cooperate with others to get things done.	☐	☐	☐
3 *Laissez faire* – leave them to get on with it, do your own thing.	☐	☐	☐
4 *Directive* – do as the boss says, be tough, control others.	☐	☐	☐
5 *Innovative* – be open, question, seek new ways and ideas.	☐	☐	☐
6 *Adaptive* – work within the frame, improve efficiency.	☐	☐	☐
7 *Competitive* – outperform your peers, be a winner.	☐	☐	☐
8 *Perfectionist* – meet impossible standards, work hard.	☐	☐	☐
9 *Achieving* – work enthusiastically to goals and plans.	☐	☐	☐
10 *Risk-avoiding* – don't take chances, mistakes are punished.	☐	☐	☐

The $64,000 question is: what do I do if the gaps are wide? As always, it all depends on the circumstances and trade-offs involved. The choices are clear:

- compromise, learn to adapt to the culture and the gap
- leave for a more congenial organisational climate
- stay and change the culture from the inside.

If you are in this predicament, do a personal cost-benefit analysis on each of the options.

The political minefields

Winning people's commitment by meeting their needs for meaning (Chapter 3) is only part of the leadership story. Before they can do that leaders must mark a path through the minefield and secure their power base.

Every organisation is a political entity. The larger it is and the more units and departments there are, the more people's goals and interests conflict. Competition is inevitable. In the promotion stakes, competition becomes tougher the higher the rank and the scarcer the senior positions.

Competition for power is at the heart of politics. And, just as power can be used in a positive or a negative way (Chapter 3), so too can politics be positive or negative. There is a difference and a choice.

The political mind-set scale

?

Test Yourself

- Where on the scale below would you place your organisation?

Negative politics		Neutral or mixed			Positive politics
1	2	3	4	5	6
☐	☐	☐	☐	☐	☐

Individual or group self-interest

- Me first, the company second
- Win-lose, dominate
- Macchiavellian

Organisational enhancement

- Honest differences of opinion
- In the company's best interest
- Ethical

- If there are negative politics how does this show itself?
- And the politics of organisational enhancement – where do you see that?
- Where does your own approach lie? Does it fit the way you want to be?

Playing negative politics is high risk. Players and company alike may suffer serious harm.

'The board of Cable and Wireless resolved the feud between Lord Young of Graffham, the executive chairman, and James Ross, the chief executive, by demanding the resignations of both yesterday ... C&W was relieved that the executive feud, which virtually paralysed the £9.6 billion company, has come to an end. Mr Olson said: "The period of uncertainty is now over. To have two senior executives not working well together was damaging to this operation in terms of reputation and what was going on inside the company."' (*The Times*, November 22, 1995)

The next day *The Times* reported a sharp rise in the share price of Cable and Wireless.

Staying out of politics is not an option. Successful leaders make it their business to succeed in the political minefield. They work their networks. They understand where power is concentrated, who can intercede effectively for whom. Who has the ear of the chief decision-makers. And who can swing extra resources. They know where the skeletons are closeted. They are sensibly cautious about taking the key stakeholders outside their comfort zones. They are good deal-makers. They don't make enemies except as a last resort.

Surviving difficult colleagues

The stressful boss
Though they spend a lot of time working at relationships, leaders have the same headaches from personality clashes as everyone else. 'Boss stress', arising from strained relations with a superior, is frequently cited as a major blight in the leader's life. Boss stress causes anxiety and reduces the leader's self-esteem and sense of competence. Being pre-occupied about the boss's negative evaluations – and the impact of this on the leader's career – will mean their mind is just not on the job. This will have little

significance or impact on the routine tasks. It is the intellectually demanding aspects of the leader's job – planning and decision-making – that really suffer.

> 'I don't want any yes-men around me: I want everyone to tell me the truth even if it costs them their jobs.'
> Sam Goldwyn

Research has shown, predictably, that more intelligent army leaders tend to show better judgement and perform better than less intelligent leaders. But this is found only when stress is low. Under high boss stress, intelligence is a handicap. Stress disrupts the ability to think and intelligent leaders come unglued in tasks that demand judgement and decisiveness.

This is exactly what happened with Pete (Chapter 2). When the temperature rose in meetings with his boss and peer, he just couldn't think straight. All he wanted to do was get out of the room. As time went by he spent more and more time doing routine work and shunned the strategic stuff. Meantime his more politically atuned colleague was spending time with the boss to his own advantage.

Boss stress has less impact on leaders who rely mostly on experience for forming judgements or making decisions. In fact, stress may give them an edge. Experience-based decisions are instinctive and intuitive. Hence they are not disrupted by stress in the way that analytic or reflective decisions are.

?

Test Yourself

- On balance, are you more inclined to apply your experience or your intellect when you tackle problems, form judgements or make decisions? Where on the scale would you place yourself?

Tend to use experience		Mixed or a balance		Tend to use intelligence	
1	2	3	4	5	6
☐	☐	☐	☐	☐	☐

- How does this tendency affect your ability to perform under stress, especially boss stress?
- Does this suggest any new ideas for coping with stress?

If you find yourself on the receiving end of boss stress:

1 Start with the axiom that most people want to do a decent job, your boss included. He/she probably doesn't realise how you feel.

2 Don't avoid your boss. Budget more time to manage upwards and plan how to use it.

3 See the world through your boss's eyes. Understand the pressures he/she is under – especially from their boss.

4 Practice saying clearly what you believe, need or want. This is being legitimately assertive.

5 Adjust your communication style to how your boss likes to communicate – top-of-the-head ideas or written business justifications, face-to-face meetings or short memos, regular meetings or by exception only.

6 Ask yourself: are you giving sufficient attention to his/her priorities?

7 Find the right opportunity to discuss openly what works best for you and him/her.

8 Assess yourself and your needs and expectations of your boss. Might you have an unrealistic expectation of authority figures?

9 Learn by closely watching others who successfully manage their relationship with your boss.

You might be part of a subordinate's stress problem without realising it. Watch out for the give-away signs around appraisal time and after any 'straight-talking' meetings. For example, when an intelligent team member starts making shaky decisions and exercising poor judgement. What you can do is to organise a meeting to share and discuss effective and satisfactory ways of working together. Another way to get the ball rolling is a programme of upward feedback from your direct reports. This can be painlessly organised through the personnel department or a consultant.

The Machiavellian type
Another stressful character who can seriously damage your leadership is the 'Mach' type. A disciple of Machiavelli, this character is shamelessly dedicated to their own interests at the expense of everyone and everything else. They do whatever it takes – deceive, cheat, use – to get their way. They are often smooth, persuasive and good at their work. They are astute at picking situations which they can twist to their advantage. They will manipulate you face-to-face when you are emotional and vulnerable. Recognise this character? The research evidence shows that it is quite common.

How to defend yourself:

- Go on the attack. Expose their tricks to others, even if it is you they have duped.
- Be sceptical of the plausible words and false promises. Watch what they do more than what they say.
- Do not make concessions. Recognise when they are stabbing you in the back and act on the knowledge.
- Avoid being with the Mach when your emotions are high. Find a reason to disengage yourself if you are going to be at a disadvantage.
- Don't make important decisions when under this person's influence. Take time to think them out independently.
- Make thorough preparations for meetings the Mach is likely to use for their own purposes. Be informed. Anticipate their proposals and tactics. Consider favourable counter-proposals you can make.

The Maverick

The third difficult colleague is the Maverick – the one who speaks out at meetings, who poses the awkward question, who refuses to toe the party line, who thinks the unthinkable, who is prepared to blow the whistle. John Harvey-Jones' advice is clear: whatever you do, listen to the Maverick. They may be your most reliable and honest information source, and the antidote to the yes-men who only tell you what you want you to hear.

Being objective about yourself

To master the complex, shifting ground that leaders occupy, you need to be as objective with yourself as you can. That means doing things that may not be your first instinct.

? Test Yourself

- In this list of survival suggestions, tick those you can put to good use.
- Circle the ones you can put into practice almost immediately.
- How are you going to apply the other items you ticked? Where and when are you going to apply them?

Survival suggestions

1 Know what you want and go for it. If you don't know where you are going any road will take you there. ☐

2 Play to your strengths, but don't overplay them or use them in the wrong situation. ☐

3 Don't rationalise your weaknesses or ignore their impact. ☐

4 Shield your weak points from view. Design jobs and situations so they won't show. Call on others who have what you lack. ☐

5 Be an outstanding listener, get people talking. ☐

6 Know the unwritten rules, learn the informal system for getting things done. ☐

7 Acknowledge that your interpretation of events is just as subjective and just as likely to be biased as others people's interpretation. ☐

8 Check your first impressions of other people's motives and intentions against the facts. ☐

9 Move out of your comfort zone – this will enable you to learn, to hear unpalatable news and feedback, and to open up festering disagreements to debate. ☐

10 Step out of your emotional armour to understand the dynamics of conflict. Step into your adversary's skin to see and feel the conflict as they do. ☐

11 When you have lost a hand, stay in the game. Accept what can't be changed. Bide your time. ☐

12 Make friends and allies, form coalitions of companionship and shared interest. Especially with your peers and even with people you do not much care for. ☐

13 Keep listening to the Mavericks, the ones who will tell you what others fear to. ☐

14 Watch out for the Machs. Don't be an easy mark for their manipulations. ☐

15 Stay in touch with reality. Set up your own intelligence conduits. Network with individuals at all levels. ☐

16 Don't underestimate or neglect your boss. You are both mutually dependant and potential allies. ☐

17 Except as a last resort, don't make enemies. Be civil to those you don't like. ☐

18 Practice self-control, don't use bad language, don't lose your cool – especially when others are present. ☐

19 Enhance your referent power – develop qualities and behaviours that others will like or admire. ☐

20 Be assertive but not aggressive. Express clearly what you want and why. Encourage others to do the same. ☐

Building your own leadership model 4

- In what sort of an organisation – size, type of business, culture, management style, personalities and players – would you be most likely to shine and feel comfortable?
- How does your present organisation measure up to this ideal?
- If you had a magic wand, which aspects of your environment would you change to better fit your style and strengths?
- What can you do to bring those changes closer?
- What is stopping you?
- How do you propose to be in the right place at the right time?

Star teams

Ordinary people doing extraordinary things

In November 1999, Scotland's football team was drawn to meet England. Everything was against the Scots. Two goals down from the first leg. Playing away from home. And, had they been English-born, not one of their players would have made the star-studded English side. But on the day, teamwork and Craig Brown, the Scottish coach, prevailed over individualism, giving the Scots a convincing millennial victory.

How did Craig Brown make a star team out of ordinary players? How do leaders enable ordinary people to do extraordinary things? Charisma is the easy answer but the wrong one. (No one has ever accused Craig Brown of being charismatic.) There are, of course, no easy answers, though we do know some of the practical things that good leaders do to make star teams.

The topics covered are:

- Teams and teamworking – why they matter
- Key actions to make star teams
- Teambuilding for fulfilment leaders
- Teambuilding for integration leaders
- Teambuilding for visionary leaders

'What's wrong with being a boring kind of guy?'
George Bush when president of the United States

Teams – the key to success

A 'team' is a small group of people working together, pooling their talents and sharing responsibility in the pursuit of an agreed goal. 'Teamworking' refers to individuals and groups working together in reasonable co-operation and harmony. Both are highly rated because:

- They are an effective means for pooling individuals' talents and skills.
- Teamworking increases cooperation and communication within and between parts of the organisation.
- Task forces and teams often solve many problems more effectively and more quickly than individuals or hierarchies.
- Teams working across organisational boundaries (e.g. product development teams) coordinate and integrate the efforts of separate functions and departments.
- Participation in the team increases people's commitment to the implementation of its decisions.
- Being accepted within a team enhances the individual's sense of identity and belonging.

When teams don't work

Teams may not live up to these promises for several reasons.

- Resistance to teams – people in hierarchies often perceive teamworking as a threat to their control.
- The wrong team for the task – like fielding a chess team to play baseball.
- Individualism – everyone is trying for goal, no one is passing the ball.

- Some people are not up to it – wrongly selected, they are there for the wrong reasons.
- Unclear goals or process, going around in circles – endless meetings.
- Competition and conflict between members.
- Consultants call all the shots – as in business process engineering.
- Conflict between teams – turf wars.
- Frustration, low morale – because of all of the above.
- The team just doesn't deliver – because of all of the above.

And lastly, using a team is sometimes the *least* effective way to get things done. A single individual may have all the required knowledge and expertise to do it by herself. Or the task may be quite simple and involving a team would just confuse the issue. It all depends on the situation.

What leaders do to make star teams

This section synthesises the actions that will transform groups of individuals into star teams. They are:

1 winning outside support for the team
2 building a structure for the team to deal effectively with its tasks
3 instilling a purpose that inspires the team
4 warming the climate within the team
5 developing effective processes for working together
6 building useful connections of shared interest, inside and outside the team.

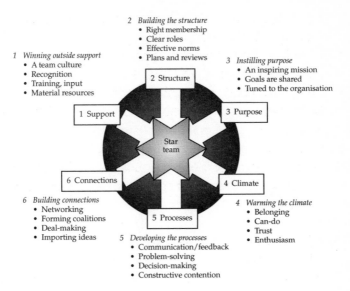

2 *Building the structure*
- Right membership
- Clear roles
- Effective norms
- Plans and reviews

1 *Winning outside support*
- A team culture
- Recognition
- Training, input
- Material resources

3 *Instilling purpose*
- An inspiring mission
- Goals are shared
- Tuned to the organisation

6 *Building connections*
- Networking
- Forming coalitions
- Deal-making
- Importing ideas

5 *Developing the processes*
- Communication/feedback
- Problem-solving
- Decision-making
- Constructive contention

4 *Warming the climate*
- Belonging
- Can-do
- Trust
- Enthusiasm

1 *Winning outside support*

- *A team culture*. Teamworking needs to become a way of life within the larger organisation. It needs to be espoused and supported by all the leaders in the organisation.
- *Recognition from the organisation*. As team spokesperson you ensure that the organisation recognises the team's mission and rewards its contributions. You nurture two-way communication between the team and other parts of the organisation.
- *Training, input*. You identify and secure whatever training and coaching the team requires to work effectively and to achieve its mission.
- *Material resources*. You identify and secure whatever other resources are required to accomplish the mission.

2 Building the structure

- *The right membership*. The team members should bring complementary skills, information and know-how needed to complete the task. No passengers. Teams of more than eight members are often cumbersome – work in sub-teams.
- *Clear roles*. Each member needs a role to call her own and all the necessary roles need to be occupied. Common roles are: leader, note-taker, event organiser. An external facilitator can be helpful especially for conflict resolution. Roles may rotate – including the leadership.
- *Effective norms*. A team should have 'rules' – how the members wish to manage themselves. Rules are about being on time, everyone having their say, being open, no hidden agendas, and so on. These are the *team's* rules, not yours.
- *Plans and reviews*. Resist the temptation to dive into projects and tasks. Have a plan to follow and systematic ways of tackling the task. Follow each meeting with a ten-minute review of how you worked as a team.

3 Instilling purpose

- *Inspiring mission*. Spell out the reason why the team exists. Use it to switch people on. For routine operations this is difficult but not impossible. Remember the floor sweeper who was 'helping to put a man on the moon' (Chapter 3).
- *Shared goals*. Commitment and consensus are vastly stronger where everyone buys into the same goals. All noses are pointed in the same direction.
- *The purpose is well understood*. Make the mission and

goals easy to grasp. Everyone understands what the purpose is. Take whatever time it takes to win understanding and commitment. Telling is not sufficient – it requires two-way dialogue.

- *In tune with the organisation's mission*. The team's mission and goals need to be in harmony with and support the organisation's vision.

4 Warming the climate

- *Belonging*. If people don't feel they belong, you don't have a team. Don't exclude them from meetings without very good reason. Involve them in the plans and the future of the team. Use including words. Hold away days to celebrate being a team.
- *Can-do*. 'Efficacy' – the feeling that we as a team can do it – is a key to high performance. Build that feeling. Put down markers to measure and celebrate the team's successes.
- *Trust.* Openness means speaking out, people saying what they really think and feel. But it is a risk. It makes the speaker vulnerable. So you as leader need to remove the risk by creating conditions for trust.
- *Enthusiasm*. This is the hallmark of high-performance teams. It is a product of all of the above.

5 Developing the processes

- *Communication/feedback*. Develop good habits of sharing information, news and ideas. Give people open access to information. Encourage the giving of feedback.
- *Problem-handling.* Have useful procedures and techniques to facilitate problem analysis and solution. Understand the pitfalls of group think.

- *Decision-making*. Have useful routines for this too.
- *Constructive contention*. Good teams practice and encourage constructive approaches to conflict. They use conflict to improve decisions and solutions. Show the way, lead by example.

6 Building connections
- *Networking*. Developing good relationships within and outside the larger organisation brings knowledge, advice and opportunities to the team. The team can also use its networks to shape opinion.
- *Forming coalitions.* By coming together with others of similar views and interest the members of a team can influence direction and decisions. The coalition members may be from within the team or with others outside the team.
- *Deal-making.* Having good outside connections enables the team to negotiate advantageous deals.
- *Importing ideas.* Many good ideas used by teams come from outside its ranks.

Teambuilding for fulfilment leaders

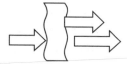

Fulfilment leaders use teambuilding and teamworking to:

- develop stable work teams
- manage projects within a department
- lead temporary teams of specialists on assignments (e.g. auditors)

- organise temporary teams of generalists (e.g. fund-raising group of parents)
- lead action units (e.g. an army patrol).

The SuperGlass Factory
This is a small, innovative and outstandingly successful specialist glass business. It has been purchased by one of the national glass companies. Bernard (first met in Chapter 1) has been put in as the production manager. Conflict runs high and morale is low in the production area. With an MBA under his belt, Bernard knows about the theory of team development and teamworking. So an away day for the team leaders and production planning staff is duly scheduled and the obligatory t-shirts are printed. Bernard asks for your views on this proposed programme.

- 'Hopes and aspirations for SuperGlass' – a slide show presentation from Bernard.
- 'Turbulent times in the construction industry' – an hour's educational input again from Bernard.
- Break-out groups to discuss the implications for SuperGlass.
- 'Why teams are needed in business' – an hour's presentation by a management consultant.
- 'Technical developments in specialist glass' – a presentation by the company's guru.
- Break-out groups to discuss the product implications for SuperGlass.

? Test Yourself

- Which key actions are missing from his plan in terms of the star team model?
- How would you redesign the away day for Bernard and why would you do it that way?

The teambuilding day might be redesigned along these lines. Bracketed numbers refer to the key actions detailed above for the star team.

- A short introduction from Bernard highlighting the parent company's support for SuperGlass (1).
- A light-hearted team game as an ice-breaker (4).
- Discussions in pairs, then in the full group, of what people want from the day (4, 5).
- The management team developing and agreeing a set of norms/rules for itself (2).
- Each member preparing and then presenting to the team achievements that have put the 'super' into SuperGlass (4).
- Break-out groups deliberating on what would restore the SuperGlass spirit and success (3).
- The break-out groups report back to everyone, then a discussion and agreement of where to go next (2).

Teambuilding for integration leaders

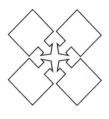

Integration leaders are key links in complex webs of diverging interests, of internal and external relationships. They use teambuilding and teamworking to:

- bring together individuals and departments that have diverging interests to secure alignment and agreement of their objectives and processes
- implement significant cross-functional changes, such as restructuring or new business processes
- form and reform temporary teams that work across organisation boundaries
- form mutual interest groups with customers, suppliers and competitors – partnering
- coordinate loose collections of individuals coming from different organisations.

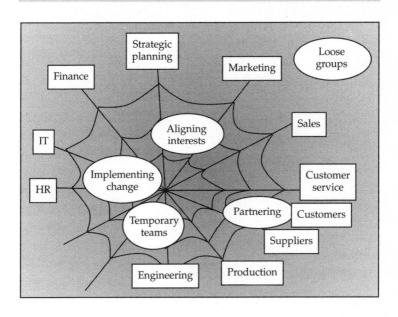

Pete

Pete the marketing manager appeared in earlier chapters. Linda his boss is rather a bully. Because the business has been reorganised, Pete now has to work much more closely with the operations manager Owen. He finds Owen abrasive and political and until then has avoided him like the plague. In the shuffle, some staff members have been transferred from one team to the other. Business processes and product development issues have not yet been resolved between the teams. Some staff members are drafting their CVs. Pete himself has been applying for jobs elsewhere.

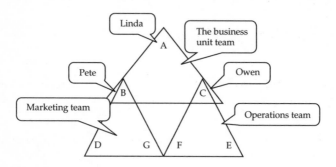

? Test Yourself

- If you were advising Pete, which star team actions would you recommend?
- And how would you suggest putting them into effect?

Your suggestions to Pete might be to:

- Take advice from HR and from senior 'grey heads' in the organisation. Explore the availability of training in managing change and of a facilitator to provide assistance (1).
- Make a persuasive case for developing a mission and shared goals for the whole business unit. And for engaging staff in the process (2).

- Raise the profile of the business process and product development issues. Emphasise the importance of having a sensible collaborative process for tackling them. Promote the idea of 'constructive contention' and its benefits (5).
- Secure support for involving and training the recently transferred team members (1).
- Have an away day for your team including an overnight for socialising and dining together (2).

Integration – facilitation skills

Integration leaders often have referent power but no position authority. Telling is not an option. They must be able to exercise facilitation skills. Facilitating is the opposite of dictating. It means making it easier for the team to work well and achieve its task. It is about enabling everyone in the group to be responsible for the team's performance and output. Facilitation is easier for Guide leaders and harder for directive, task-oriented leaders – particularly Heroes who want to run the show.

If teams are not used to a facilitating approach, it will take time, practice, patience and perseverance before they take to it. If they are in a directing (power) culture and used to Hero leadership, it will be even harder. They will be expecting to be told what to do next and what to think. So when you don't do that, they will become frustrated. Training for the whole team on this new style of leading greatly accelerates the learning process.

? Test Yourself

- Tick off the skills you know you already use.
- Of the remainder, circle the three or four that would be most useful for you to develop.

Facilitation skills	*Comments and questions*
☐ Involve the team in planning the meeting.	'Let me know what you want on the agenda. Will you lead on that item?'
☐ Help the team have a full grasp of the facts – as opposed to opinion.	'Can you take us through what happened step by step so we can all understand the situation.'
☐ Encourage specifics. Generalities lead to misunderstanding.	'I think I understand – but can you give an example?'
☐ Help the team explore the underlying causes.	'What do you think the underlying problem is? What's your analysis of why it happened?'
☐ Get the team back on track by clarifying the process.	'We seem to be getting our analyses and solutions all mixed up. Let's be sure we do a sound analysis first.'
☐ Provide structure. Keep the team on target with its time.	'We have five more minutes to look at the options, then we must take a decision.'
☐ Give everyone an opportunity to contribute.	'Take just a minute to jot down your own thoughts on the issue, then we'll go round the table.'

Facilitation skills	*Comments and questions*
☐ Provide encouragement.	'I think we should be pleased with how far we have come today.'
☐ Teach to need – when you have a skill or knowledge that would help at a particular point.	'We seem to be stuck on how to reach a decision. Let me explain a useful technique...'
☐ 'Reframe' – help the group see an event in another way to expand their thinking and understanding.	'Let's look at it from the perspective of the supplier. Where are they coming from, do you think?'
☐ Get underlying doubts and conflicts on the table.	'Let's go back over that decision one more time – just in case there are any doubts.'

Teambuilding for visionary leaders

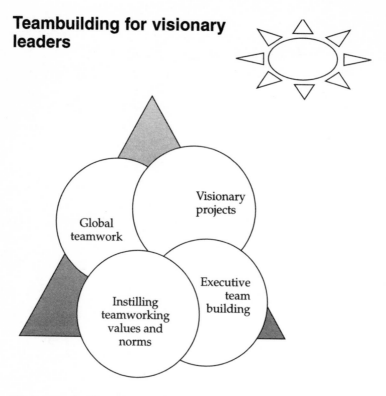

Visionary leaders use teambuilding and teamworking to:

- instil team values and norms throughout the organisation – cutting across or cutting out hierarchies
- build a strong executive team – balancing the robust individualism of high achievers with a mutual respect and commitment to the collective purpose
- develop global networks across national frontiers –

respecting cultural differences and local conditions, accumulating and duplicating best practice
- steer visionary development projects that could have radical impact on the market.

Drum Label Group

DLG is privately owned and has five operating companies that supply adhesive, woven and special labels to consumer goods producers and retailers. The companies have been managed as separate entities, the managing directors only ever meeting at the Group's annual social. However, David, the chief executive, can see the commercial benefit of pooling the Group's know-how. He proposes a network of cross-company expert teams and centres of excellence. None of the managing directors are enthusiastic. Three compete in the same markets. There is bad blood between two of them over a key account. And all, being strongly independent characters, resent head office 'interference'. David engages a consultant to plan and facilitate a three-day teambuilding meeting with the managing directors.

? **Test Yourself**

- If you were David's consultant, which star team actions would you recommend?
- And how would you suggest putting them into effect?

These are possible actions one might recommend:

- Hold an initial half-day meeting with the managing directors to outline the pooling concept and the possible applications. Give them opportunity to give you feedback – hear their objections without defending (5).

- Out of the head office budget provide training courses in teambuilding, teamworking and handling change. Mix company personnel on the courses. Provide consulting support to the cross-company expert teams (1).
- Use the training courses to generate interest and enthusiasm at all levels of the operating companies (4).
- Give the managing directors places on all first courses 'so that they can check them out' (4).
- Lobby the managing directors and the technical directors individually. Discuss their objections. Build coalitions of supporters (6).
- Only then hold the three-day meeting with the managing directors. And expect the development of the team to take time.

'When workers identify with a leadership style that offers conceptual strength, firm direction, and sensitivity to their feelings, they in turn operate in and become teachers of that style.'
Levinson, 1988

Building your own leadership model 5

- Do you see any opportunities for introducing or improving teambuilding or teamworking?
- What possible benefits could come from these opportunities?
- How specifically can you put the star team ideas to work for your team?
- Which team skills do you propose to use and which do you want to develop?

Aspirations for the future

Positioning yourself

Testing your leadership skills is an ongoing process. Positioning yourself for the future – for its challenges and opportunities – is equally necessary. This chapter invites you to:

- look upstream at what the future might hold
- explore possible implications for the leadership you will be required to give
- develop a vision of yourself as a leader.

'Everything is up for grabs. All the things we used to take for granted about our organisations – the markets we were in, who our customers were, our competitors – need to be questioned.'
Sir Iain Vallance, Chairman of BT

Looking to the future is a chancy business. Thomas Watson, when chairman of IBM, supposed that 'there's a world market for maybe five computers'. Today, some sixty years on, there are many millions of computers in the world. In 1981, Microsoft's Bill Gates prophesied with similar foresight that '640K (RAM) ought to be enough for anybody'. Today's entry-level PCs have a hundred times that amount. These mistaken prophecies are forgivable, for the world is increasingly turbulent and turbulent means unpredictable. No organisation – business, church, school, government body, university or charity – can take its future for granted. Marks and Spencer has toppled off its high-street pedestal. Oxbridge have fallen behind in the premier league of world universities.

Leadership 2000 – best guesses

Though the future of leadership is equally unpredictable, there are some strong indications about what we can expect.

1 *Distributing leadership.* Organisations will probably need more leadership and more leaders because:
   - Centralised authoritarian forms of organisation are going the way of the dinosaur. Team-based organisations and 'networked organisations' – flatter, looser and relationship-based – are taking their place.
   - Staff know much more than their managers can ever know. The thrust will be to enable them, not to control them.
   - To satisfy customer requirements, frontline staff need to be empowered to develop delivery strategies and make on-the-spot decisions.

   Implications. These trends mean that solitary leaders simply won't be able to know it all or control it all. Leadership will need to be shared ever more widely. Every staff member will be a potential fulfilment leader.

2 *Leadership qualities, style and images.*
   The near future will call on certain qualities more than others.
   - A balance of task and consideration leadership will continue to be required by those you lead. These are probably universal needs, though the strength of the

needs will depend on the experience and independence of the follower.

- The increasing volume of information is both a boon and a bane. It makes focusing more difficult but more necessary. The successful leaders will be those who identify their most critical leadership tasks – probably two or three – and keep these constantly at the centre of their attention and priorities. They will develop mechanisms for gathering intelligence about significant events, risks and ideas – and for filtering the masses of data coming at them.
- Globalisation is bringing a vastly greater mixture of cultures into our businesses and workplaces. Cultural diversity is becoming a fact of life. Successful leaders will be the ones who are sensitive to differences between peoples. They will question the accepted wisdom of their own culture, and show humility and respect when working with people from other cultures.
- Entrepreneurial thinking grounded in industry and market knowledge will be crucial for business leaders. Every successful leader will have to be internet literate.
- If the Guide is one of your preferred images, you will be especially valued because you have the potential to knit diverse organisations into integrated wholes.

Implications. These indications offer clear signposts for self-development to tomorrow's leaders.

3 *Winning people's commitment*.
The emerging power of employees is colossal. While

demand for knowledge workers increases, supplies of young people coming into the job market are shrinking. The last decades of the twentieth century were about delighting the customer. The first decade of the twenty-first will be about attracting employees. People will insist on being treated as individuals and not as an anonymous collective. Flatter organisations mean fewer opportunities for using promotion as an incentive.

Implications. Reward power and position power will carry less and less weight and referent power will carry more. More of the leader's energies must be spent winning their followers' commitment and ensuring that key staff remain with the organisation.

4 *The right place at the right time*.
   The future is not just more of the same.
   - Electronic commerce is altering retailing and customer services beyond all recognition. Order your groceries on the Internet and Tesco will deliver them next day. Online companies offer unprecedented ranges of product and instant expert advice. With the web as shop window and order taker, new back-bedroom enterprises are competing head-to-head with established businesses. Computing and communication technologies have made the virtual organisation a reality.
   - Organisations are entering into interesting but complex relationships – supplier partnerships, joint ventures and joint-marketing, shared R and D, cross-licensing, alliances with competitors.
   - Organisations outgrow their leaders. The greater the

turbulence and the faster the pace of change the
shorter is the leader's shelf life.

> '*Once successful, a manager changes thinking and
> action only after great resistance. Behaviour that has
> been rewarded in the past will be repeated in the
> present and future.*'
> Abraham Zaleznik

Implications. Leaders will have to question and resist
replicating what worked for them in the past. They
must keep informed of what is going on in the
broad environment outside their organisations. They
need to spend time outside their organisation
looking in, learning to see it as suppliers,
competitors, customers, potential customers and
staff see it. If you are an integration leader, you will
build connections with other organisations, not just
within your own organisation. Mature leaders will
recognise when they are no longer being effective
and move on. They will find a satisfying challenge
for their talents elsewhere.

5 *Building star teams*
Two further reasons why you as a leader need to be a
developer of teams:
- First, the power of the team will be more vital than ever
  in terms of innovation. Each member of a team will
  spend at least twenty per cent of their time developing
  and implementing new ideas. The first step will be to
  organise work to find that time for innovation.
- Second, teams are becoming more widely dispersed
  and so more difficult to develop. The world is

shrinking. National barriers to trade are falling. Computing and telecommunication technologies are spreading. The free market rules.

Implications. Leaders will need to redefine their roles – from being the source of good ideas to being a catalyst for the team's ideas. And from being crisis managers to those who make it possible for their teams to think and innovate. A further emerging challenge is to build teams at a distance across national and political boundaries from scratch and quickly.

'The job is not to impose yesterday's normal on a changed today; but to change the business, its behaviour, its attitudes, its expectations – as well as its products, its markets, and its distribution channels – to fit the new realities.'
Peter Drucker

Pause for thought

- Which of these predictions are most relevant for you?
- How can you position yourself best?
- What might you influence your organisation to do more of or less of, or do differently?
- What self-development might you need?
- What development might your organisation need?
- What positioning steps do you need to take *now*?

The last word is yours

'Eventually you rely on your ideal, and the picture in your mind of the sort of person you would like to be, and would like to remain. I think it is necessary to have this idealistic portrait to which you can aspire, tucked away where you can check up to see how far, like Dorian Gray, you are altering.'
John Harvey-Jones, former chairman of ICI.

The aim of this little book has been to highlight the picture in your mind of the leader you would like to be. Take some time to look back at the thoughts and insights it has stimulated. Not just the influencing skills and the self-presentation skills, but the inner drives, the inner values and what image of leadership you want to make your own. The sum total of what being a leader means to you. What are the four or five most telling points you will take away?

And finally, what epitaph would you like to have as a leader? What would you want your followers to say about you when you move on? This is worth thinking about, because that will be the vision to guide you in your onward development in the art of leadership.

'The best of all leaders is the one who helps people so that, eventually, they don't need him. Then comes the one they love and admire. Then comes the one they fear. The worst is the one who lets people push him around. Where there is no trust, people will act in bad faith. The best leader doesn't say much, but what he

says carries weight. When he is finished with his work, the people say, "It happened naturally." '
Lao Tzu, Chinese philosopher, 6th century BC

Sources and references

Chapter 1

Garfield, C., *Peak Performers*, New York: Avon Books, 1987.
Hesselbein, F., 'The "How to Be" Leader', in Hesselbein, F.,
Goldsmith, M. and Beckhard, R. (eds), *Leader of the Future*,
New York: Jossey-Bass, 1996.

Chapter 2

Kouzes, J. M. and Posner, B. Z., *The Leadership Challenge*, San
Francisco: Jossey-Bass, 1985.
The Least Preferred Co-worker Scale is adapted from
Fiedler, F. E., *A Theory of Leadership Effectiveness*, New York:
McGraw Hill, 1967.

For information about the 'Images of Leadership'
questionnaire and interpretative materials contact:
The Innovative Management Partnership
Abbeyfield House
15 Abington Park Crescent
Northampton
England NN3 3AD

Chapter 3

McClelland, D. C., Retrospective Commentary to
McClelland, D. C. and Burnham, D. H., 'Power is the Great
Motivator' reprinted in *Harvard Business Review*, 126–139,
January–February 1995.

There are many useful publications on the Myers–Briggs
model of preferences and types. Try Myers, I. B. *Introduction
to Type*, Fifth Edition, Palo Alto: Consulting Psychologists

Press, 1993 and Oxford Psychologists Press, 1993. Also
Kummerow, J. M., Barger, N. J. and Kirby, L. K., *Work Types*,
New York: Warner, 1997. Information about questionnaires
used to measure Myers–Briggs preferences can be obtained
in the UK from: Oxford Psychologists Press Ltd, Lambourne
House, 311-321 Banbury Road, Oxford OX2 7JH.

Maccoby, M., *The Leader*, New York: Simon & Schuster,
1981.
Schlesinger, L. A. and Balzer, R. J., 'An alternative to
buzzword management: the culture-performance link',
Personnel, 62 (9), 1985.

Chapter 4

For an interesting development of the idea that organisation
life cycle is related to adaptive-innovative thinking styles,
consult Vicere, A. A., 'The Strategic Leadership Imperative
for Executive Development', *Human Resource Planning*, 15
(1), 15–31, 1992.

One of the best expositions of the interaction between boss
stress and intelligence is Fiedler, F. E and Link, T. G.,
'Leader intelligence, interpersonal stress, and task
performance', in Sternberg, R. J. and Wagner, R. K. (eds),
Mind in Context, Cambridge: Cambridge University Press,
1994.

For further information on the Mach personality, consult
Christie, R. and Geis, F. L. (eds), *Studies in Machiavellianism*,
New York: Academic Press, 1970.
Kirton, M.J., 'A theory of cognitive style', in M. Kirton (ed.),
*Adaptors and Innovators: Styles of creativity and problem-
solving*, Revised Edition, London: Routledge, 1994.

Chapter 5

There are many excellent books on teamworking and teambuilding. One of the finest is Bradford, D. L. and Cohen, A. R., *Managing for Excellence*, New York: Wiley, 1984.
Levinson, H., *The Exceptional Executive*, Cambridge, Mass.: Harvard University Press, 1968.

Chapter 6

Drucker, P., *Managing for Results*, New York: Harper & Row, 1964.
Harvey-Jones, J., *Making it Happen*, London: Collins, 1988.
Vallance, I, 'In my opinion', *Management Today*, 14, December 1999.
Zaleznik, A., *The Managerial Mystique*, New York: Harper & Row, 1989.

Further *Test Your ...* titles from Hodder & Stoughton and the Institute of Management, all at £6.99

0 340 78005 3	Test Your Aptitude & Ability	❏
0 340 78006 1	Test Your Personality	❏
0 340 78050 9	Test Your Management Style	❏
0 340 78169 6	Test Your Management Skills	❏

Publishing in September 2000:

0 340 78287 0	Test Your Financial Awareness	❏
0 340 78288 9	Test Your Literacy	❏
0 340 78289 7	Test Your Numeracy	❏
0 340 78290 0	Test Your Potential	❏

All Hodder & Stoughton books are available from your local bookshop or can be ordered direct from the publisher. Just tick the titles you want and fill in the form below. Prices and availability subject to change without notice.

To: Hodder & Stoughton Ltd, Cash Sales Department, Bookpoint, 78 Milton Park, Abingdon, Oxon OX14 4TD. If you have a credit card you may order by
telephone – 01235 400414
          fax – 01235 400454
E-mail address: orders@bookpoint.co.uk

Please enclose a cheque or postal order made payable to Bookpoint Ltd to the value of the cover price and allow the following for postage and packaging:

UK & BFPO: £4.30 for one book; £6.30 for two books; £8.30 for three books.

OVERSEAS & EIRE: £4.80 for one book; £7.10 for 2 or 3 books (surface mail).

Name: ....

Address: ....

....

....

If you would prefer to pay by credit card, please complete:

Please debit my Visa/Mastercard/Diner's Card/American Express (delete as appropriate) card no:

❏ ❏ ❏ ❏ ❏ ❏ ❏ ❏ ❏ ❏ ❏ ❏ ❏ ❏ ❏ ❏

Signature .... Expiry date ....